MATH
GRADE 6

Curriculum
for *Gifted Students*

essons, Activities, and Extensions for Gifted and Advanced Learners

Student Workbook
Sections I-II

CENTER FOR GIFTED EDUCATION
WITH JAMES M. MORONEY

William & Mary
School of Education

CENTER FOR GIFTED EDUCATION
P.O. Box 8795
Williamsburg, VA 23187

Prufrock Press Inc.
P.O. Box 8813
Waco, TX 76714-8813
Phone: (800) 998-2208
Fax: (800) 240-0333
http://www.prufrock.com

TABLE OF CONTENTS

LESSON 1.1 ACTIVITY
A Bazaar Relationship of Ratios

Directions: You and a partner are responsible for running a shop in an ancient bazaar where bartering is the main form of transaction. You will barter with the other shops in the bazaar using the agreed-upon exchange rates between objects.

Before You Begin

1. Establish an exchange rate between items. With your classmates, debate and rank the objects in the bazaar in order from least valuable to most valuable. Debate with your classmates how much of one object you would trade for an object of higher perceived value. Keep in mind the perceived value of each object in a classroom setting. For example, a sheet of paper may be considered more important than a paper clip, so you might establish an exchange rate of 10 paper clips for 1 sheet of paper (or a ratio of 10:1). This ratio might change a bit as the activity unfolds, but it will give you a good starting point when making your ratio tables.

2. Using Lesson 1.1 Bazaar Ratio Table for Exchange Rates, write the basic exchange rate for your product and other products in the market. You may use some of the ratios agreed upon during the discussion, or you might choose to alter them a bit as you see fit. Fill in the ratio table using the basic exchange rate and the equivalent exchange rates for trading multiple items. You might have something like 10 paper clips for 1 sheet of paper, so your next column in your ratio table will read 20 paper clips for 2 sheets of paper.

3. Make a shopping list of "needs" by looking at the other shops around the classroom and writing how much of each item you need. You will have to obtain these items during the bartering. Vary the amounts of the items for which you are shopping. For example, if you are shopping for two pencils, try to avoid also shopping for two erasers and two pens. Your shopping list might look like this:

Items Needed	1 piece of paper	2 erasers	20 pushpins	50 paper clips
Exchanged	1 sleeve of staples	1 sleeve of staples	1 sleeve of staples 2 erasers	5 sleeves of staples

Because you needed 20 pushpins, you exchanged one sleeve of staples and two erasers. You may not have had enough sleeves of staples to exchange for the pushpins, so you bartered with a value that was an equal amount.

During the Bartering Exchange

1. You and your partner will operate a shop in the bazaar. One of you will operate the shop, and the other will move between shops and do the bartering. You first priority as a barterer will be to obtain the "needs" from your shopping list. After about 5 minutes of bartering, you and your partner will switch roles, alternating at 5-minute intervals. Try to obtain as many items through bartering as possible. Remember that not all items will have an exact exchange rate. This is where bartering comes into play. In order to obtain the required items on your shopping list, you may need to barter with amounts that will not be an exact exchange. For example, if you need four sleeves of staples, you may need to barter with multiple items in order to complete the transaction. Look at the example below.

Items Needed	1 piece of paper	2 erasers	20 pushpins	50 paper clips
Exchanged	1 sleeve of staples	1 sleeve of staples	2 sleeves of staples	3 pieces of paper 4 erasers

If you need 50 paper clips to complete your shopping list, but are out of sleeves of staples, you might need to put together an equivalent offer, such as 3 pieces of paper and 4 erasers. Notice you have offered a combination of items that is of equal value to 5 sleeves of staples as shown in the chart on page 9. In some cases, you may need to offer more than the value of the item in order to make sure you complete your shopping list.

2. Move through the marketplace and barter with other shop owners by exchanging your items with them for other items. You may also barter with other shoppers instead of the merchants if you feel that you can get a better deal for an item you need. Write down the exchange ratio for each transaction that you make. You will need this exchange ratio when completing your end-of-day ratio tables.

3. At your shop, record all transactions you make on Lesson 1.1 Bazaar Ratio Table for Exchange Rates. You should vary the number of your item that you are exchanging. For example, if one of your customers barters for two of your item, no other customer may barter for two of your item.

After the Exchange

1. You must run an end-of-day operation to record all transactions throughout the day.

2. Complete Lesson 1.1 Bazaar End-of-Day Graphing Worksheet by plotting the ratio table that shows the relationship between your product and the other products in the bazaar. You must graph both the original ratio tables you came up with at the beginning of the activity and the actual ratios you used while bartering. Graph each of the ratio tables and compare them.

3. With other groups, compare exchanges you may have made using other items besides paper clips to establish a common ratio between items based on that day's sales. For example, if one person exchanged 3 erasers for 6 pencils and another person exchanged 3 erasers for 4 pencils, the class may decide that the appropriate ratio is 3 erasers for 5 pencils.

4. Justify two of your transactions using ratio language. For example, 2 pencils were bartered for 8 erasers because every pencil is equivalent to 4 erasers. You could also say because an eraser is worth 2 paper clips and a ruler is worth 7 paper clips, we decided to exchange 4 erasers for 1 ruler to get as close to the ratio as possible while meeting the needs of our list.

Extend Your Thinking

1. Discuss with your partner the advantages and disadvantages of using a bartering system where buyers and sellers exchange items based on a ratio of perceived value. List two or three advantages and disadvantages on a piece of paper.

2. A new culture discovers your bazaar and wants to begin trading with an item you have never seen before. How could you and the other shopkeepers determine a fair way to set a value for the new item? You and the other shopkeepers can take turns bartering with the new item and establish a ratio between the new item and your product. How can you use ratios to establish a common value for the new item? Answer on a separate piece of paper.

3. Discuss what it may have been like when two unfamiliar cultures met for the first time (list examples on another piece of paper). How might these two cultures have determined the value of items and goods that were unfamiliar to them before they decided to start trading?

LESSON 1.1 ACTIVITY
Bazaar Ratio Table for Exchange Rates

Directions: As you and your classmates establish exchange rates, you and your partner should fill in the ratio table that represents the exchange ratio that you want between your item and all of the other items in the bazaar. Then fill in a similar table that shows the actual ratio between items that you traded while bartering.

Table 1: Exchange Ratio

Your Item: _____

Bazaar item: _____

Your Item	Bazaar Item

Table 1: Actual Ratio

Your Item: _____

Bazaar item: _____

Your Item	Bazaar Item

Table 2: Exchange Ratio

Your Item: _____

Bazaar item: _____

Your Item	Bazaar Item

Table 2: Actual Ratio

Your Item: _____

Bazaar item: _____

Your Item	Bazaar Item

Table 3: Exchange Ratio	
Your Item: _____	
Bazaar item: _____	
Your Item	**Bazaar Item**

Table 3: Actual Ratio	
Your Item: _____	
Bazaar item: _____	
Your Item	**Bazaar Item**

Table 4: Exchange Ratio	
Your Item: _____	
Bazaar item: _____	
Your Item	**Bazaar Item**

Table 4: Actual Ratio	
Your Item: _____	
Bazaar item: _____	
Your Item	**Bazaar Item**

Section I: Ratios and Proportional Relationships

Table 5: Exchange Ratio

Your Item: _____

Bazaar item: _____

Your Item	Bazaar Item

Table 5: Actual Ratio

Your Item: _____

Bazaar item: _____

Your Item	Bazaar Item

Table 6: Exchange Ratio

Your Item: _____

Bazaar item: _____

Your Item	Bazaar Item

Table 6: Actual Ratio

Your Item: _____

Bazaar item: _____

Your Item	Bazaar Item

LESSON 1.1
Bazaar End-of-Day Graphing Worksheet

Directions: Now is the time to run an "end-of-day" closing for your time in the bazaar. On each graph below, plot the original ratio table that you established prior to beginning the bartering. Then, for the same item, plot the actual values that were exchanged during the bartering. Draw a line for each graph and compare the two. Do this for all of the different items for which you bartered during your day in the bazaar.

GRAPH 1

Exchange between _____ and _____ .

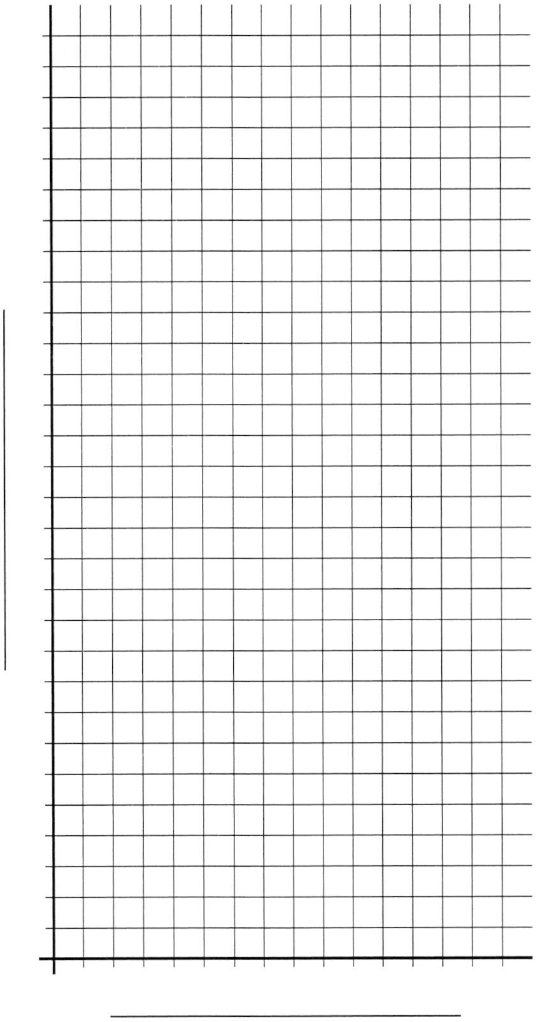

GRAPH 2

Exchange between _____ and _____ .

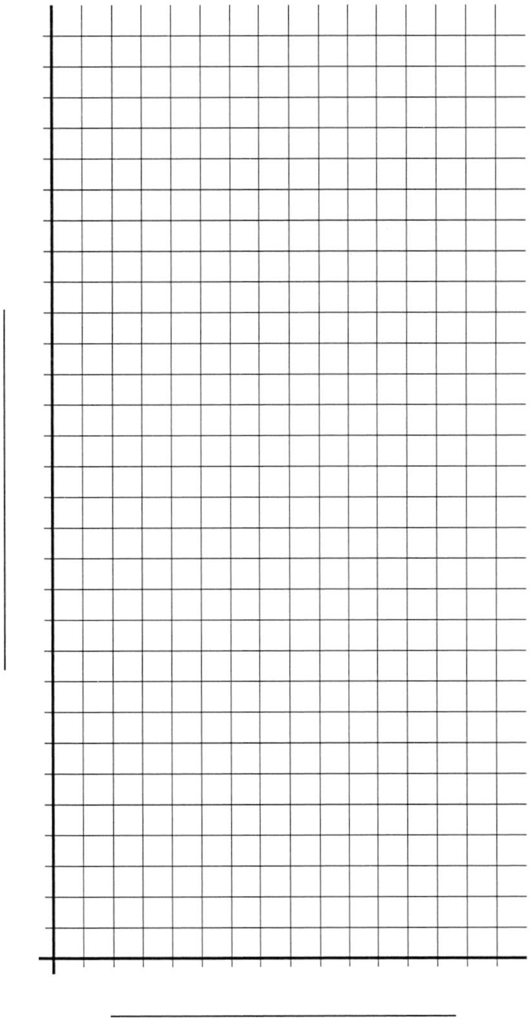

GRAPH 3

Exchange between _____
and _____ .

GRAPH 4

Exchange between _____
and _____ .

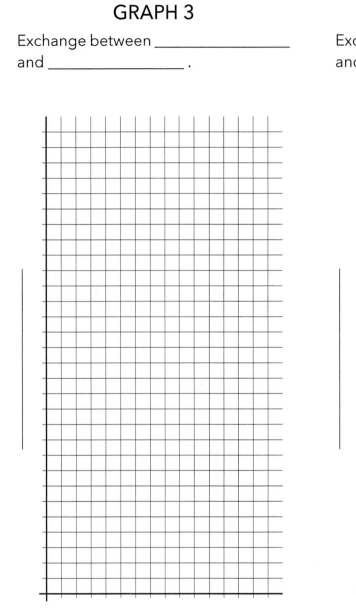

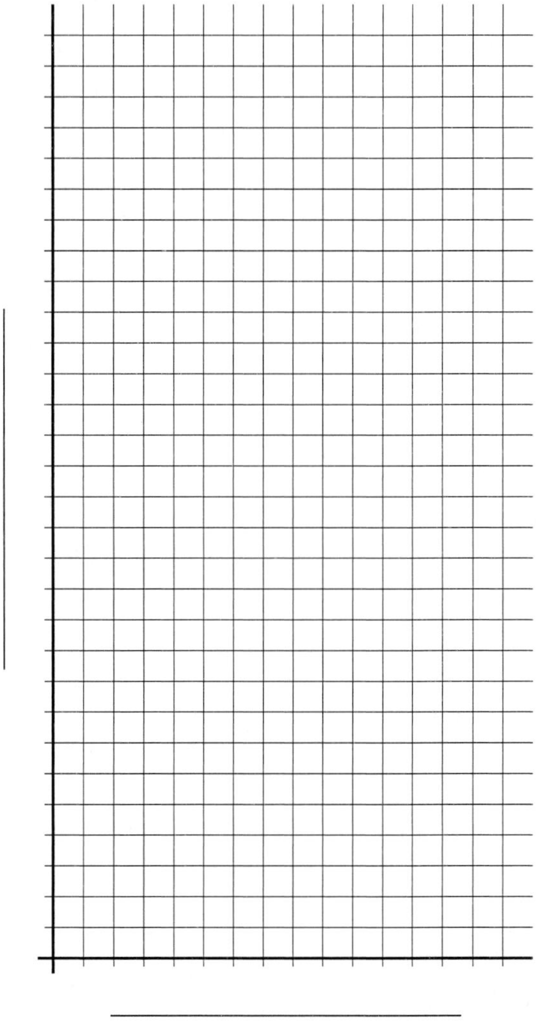

GRAPH 5

Exchange between _____
and _____ .

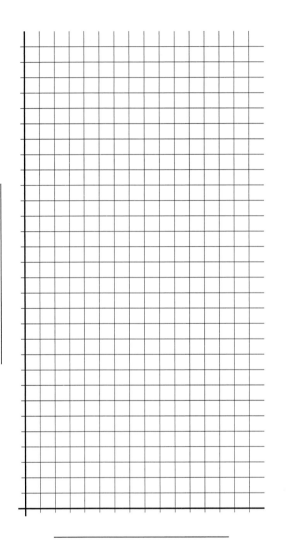

_____

GRAPH 6

Exchange between _____
and _____ .

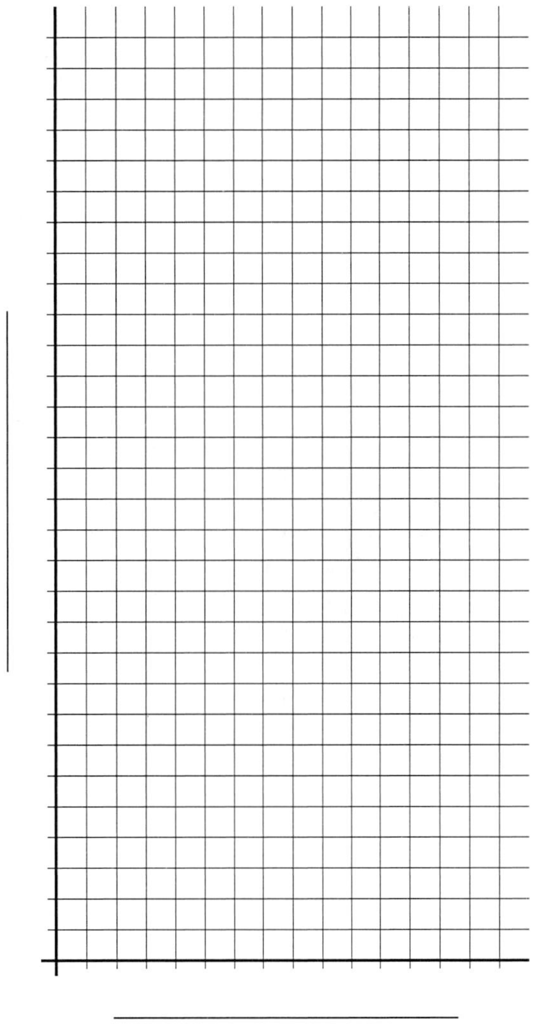

_____

LESSON 1.1 PRACTICE
Using Ratios

Directions: Complete the problems below.

1. Jessica received a flyer for a new middle school that was opening in her neighborhood. The flyer stated that the ratio of teachers to students in all classrooms is 1:9. Jessica thought, "If there are four sixth-grade classrooms, there must be 32 students in the sixth grade."

   a. Is Jessica correct in her statement?

   b. Create a ratio table that proves your answer to Part A.

Classroom(s)				
Teachers				
Students				

   c. If you were Jessica's friend, how would you explain her mistake and teach her how to correct it?

   d. If the sixth-grade class has 4 classrooms, the seventh-grade class has 6 classrooms, and the eighth-grade class has 5 classrooms, how many total students are in the school? Show your calculations.

2. The ratio of women to total passengers on a ship is 3:8.

   a. If each part of the ratio represents 50 people, how many women are on board the ship and how many total passengers are on the ship?

b. Based on the numbers in Part A, how many total men are on the ship?

c. Write a simplified ratio for the number of women to men.

d. An additional 200 people board the ship. The ratio of the new passengers is 7 men for every 3 women. With the additional passengers included, what is the new ratio of men to women?

3. A local market encourages vendors to use bartering to buy and sell products. Monique talks with a man who is willing to exchange 25 beads for 6 of Monique's bracelets.
   a. If Monique gives him 18 bracelets, how many beads did she receive?

   b. The next vendor mentions to Monique that she usually only exchanges her ribbons for beads. "I exchange 2 ribbons for every 5 beads," she tells Monique. She notices that Monique has bracelets: "If you can figure out an exchange rate for ribbons and bracelets that is equivalent to what I exchange for beads, then we have a deal." What is an exchange ratio that Monique could offer to the ribbon vendor that would be fair?

   c. If Monique received 20 more ribbons than the number of bracelets that she gave to the vendor, how many ribbons did she receive? How many bracelets did she trade away? Use the exchange ratio from the answer to Part B.

Extend Your Thinking

1. Research the currency exchange between four different currencies from around the world (not the U.S. dollar). Make a basic exchange ratio table that compares the price of a U.S. dollar to each of the four different currencies.

2. Use the evidence in the ratio table to draw conclusions about the strength of the economy in each of the four countries.

LESSON 1.1

Assessment Practice

Directions: Complete the problems below.

1. Justin and his family visited the Audubon Zoo in New Orleans. After stopping by the monkey cages and the elephant cages, Justin realized there were 7 monkeys for every 2 elephants. If there were 10 more monkeys than elephants, how many elephants were at the zoo?
   a. 12
   b. 17
   c. 10
   d. 4

2. For a school field trip, the state law requires that there should be a ratio of 1 chaperone for every 5 students on the bus. There are currently 16 total people on the bus, with a ratio of 1 chaperone for every 3 students. How many more students can they add to the bus before going over the lawful limit?
   a. 4
   b. 5
   c. 9
   d. 15

3. A company currently has a ratio of 3 workstations for every section of the company. If the company has 5 sections and recently added 45 workstations, what is the new ratio of workstations to sections of the company?
   a. 5:1
   b. 9:1
   c. 12:1
   d. 15:1

4. The ratio of the distance traveled on a trip to the entire distance is 120:360. What is the ratio of the distance traveled to the distance remaining in the trip?
   a. 120:240
   b. 240:360
   c. 240:120
   d. 360:120

5. In a bazaar, 10 pounds of salt are worth 8 bolts of silk. If 2 bolts of silk are equal to 9 stacks of papyrus, how many pounds of salt are equal to 18 stacks of papyrus?
   a. 20
   b. 2
   c. 4
   d. 5

LESSON 1.2 ACTIVITY
Rate Your Products

Directions: You are in charge of advertising for a product that is being sold at local grocery stores. You need to make an advertisement that shares the unit price of your item compared to other competitors selling similar items.

1. Begin by choosing three different brands of the same food item. For example, chips may be considered a food item, and Lays, Pringles, and Cheetos would be three different brands of chips.

2. Calculate the unit price of the three items. Use the Lesson 1.2 Unit Price Comparison handout to show your work and explain how you found the unit price for each item.

3. Your advertisement will advertise the item that has the cheapest unit price and is the best buy.

4. Compare the product that you want to sell to its competitors. In your advertisement, you should try to highlight the strengths of your product (in this case, its unit price) and point out the weaknesses of the other products, specifically how the unit price is higher than that of your product.

5. Create a storyboard for your advertisement. Use Lesson 1.2 Advertisement Storyboard handout to assist you.

6. Present your advertisement to the class. Be sure to explain how your group calculated the unit rate and decided which purchase is the best buy.

Extend Your Thinking

1. As each group is presenting, make an observation about each group's best buy compared to the other products in that group. After all of the advertisements have been presented, discuss with a partner a pattern that you noticed among the "best buys." How can you and your partner hypothesize which products will be the best buys?

2. You are selected to appear on a food show at your local TV station. You must create a "recipe" composed of food items that were used in the activity and presented by you and your classmates. Although it may not be an actual recipe, try to think of products that might go well together in a dish. Be creative! Choose four products that were presented. Specify that the ratio of the products used in the dish needs to be 4:3:2:1. For example, if you want to make a four-layer dip, you would use 4 ounces of guacamole, 3 ounces of black beans, 2 ounces of corn, and 1 ounce of sour cream to keep the ratio 4:3:2:1. Your teacher may assign a specific amount that your recipe needs to make. Calculate the unit price of one of your recipe items by taking into account how the ratios were used.

3. You are in charge of planning a grocery list for a month in your house. Reflect on the items that each of the groups presented during the activity. Choose three items. Think of how many of each of the items you might use throughout a month. For example, if one group presents on cereal, you might use three boxes of cereal in a month. After planning out a grocery list, calculate how much you would save total by choosing the better buys in each of the categories.

LESSON 1.2
Unit Price Comparison

Directions: Choose three items that fall into the same category in a grocery store. For example, you might select three different types of soda. Identify the product and its cost. Notice what weight or volume is used to measure the product and list the amount in the space provided. Then, calculate the unit price for each of the products to see which one is the better buy.

1. **Product 1:** _____

   Cost of this product: _____

   Product is measured in: _____ (e.g., ounces, pounds, grams, liters)

   The unit price is: _____

2. **Product 2:** _____

   Cost of this product: _____

   Product is measured in: _____ (e.g., ounces, pounds, grams, liters)

   The unit price is: _____

3. **Product 3:** _____

   Cost of this product: _____

   Product is measured in: _____ (e.g., ounces, pounds, grams, liters)

   The unit price is: _____

4. How did you calculate the unit price of your products?

5. Is there another way you could have figured out the best buy without calculating the unit price?

Math Curriculum for Gifted Students, Grade 6, Sections I–II

LESSON 1.2
Advertisement Storyboard

Directions: Create an advertisement using unit prices that compares your product with two of its competitors. Advertise your product as the "best buy" by comparing it as the obvious choice over its competitors. Use mathematics as support to your argument.

1. In the boxes below, show the different unit prices as a comparison for each of the products. You may also brainstorm ways that your product is better than the other product (besides the price), so that you can use these in your advertisement.

Positive Qualities of the Best Buy	Negative Qualities of the Competitor

2. Use the squares below to brainstorm and roughly design your storyboard for your advertisement. The medium through which you present your advertisement is up to you.

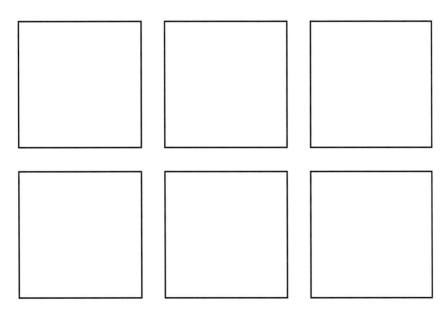

LESSON 1.2 PRACTICE
Comparing Unit Price

Directions: Complete the problems below.

1. Bob's T-Shirt Outlet recently sold 50 T-shirts for $627.50.
   a. What is the unit price for one T-shirt at Bob's T-Shirt Outlet?

   b. If each T-shirt costs Bob's T-Shirt Outlet $5.35 to make, how much profit did the store make with its order of 50 shirts?

   c. If Bob's T-Shirt Outlet sells 250 shirts every week, how much money did the store make over a 3-week period? How much of that money was profit?

2. A competitor, Quality Shirts, opens down the street. It wants to sell better quality shirts for a cheaper price than Bob's T-Shirt Outlet. It costs the store $7.75 to make each shirt, and they sell each shirt for $11.90.
   a. How much profit does Quality Shirts make per shirt?

   b. How many shirts would Quality Shirts have to sell to earn more **profit** than Bob's T-Shirt Outlet?

c. Quality Shirts has to set aside $500 a week from its profits in order to stay open for business. This cost includes employee salaries, electricity bills, and building rent. Fahad, the owner of Quality Shirts, wants to know how many shirts he needs to sell in order to earn enough profit to put $1,000 in the bank each week. Considering the $500 overhead, how many shirts will he need to sell each week?

Extend Your Thinking

1. Choose a recipe from Allrecipes.com or another website of your choice. Determine the total cost of making the meal by using the prices for each of the ingredients in the recipe. Explain how to figure out the price per serving of the recipe based on the number of people it serves and the total cost to make the meal.

LESSON 1.2

Assessment Practice

Directions: Complete the problems below.

1. Diner Doughnuts sells a dozen doughnuts for $3.96. Bargain Do-nuts sells 3 dough-nuts for $0.93. How much money would a customer save if he bought a dozen doughnuts from Bargain Do-nuts instead of Diner Doughnuts?
   a. $0.15
   b. $0.24
   c. $0.28
   d. $1.24

2. Ben has a 20-gallon tank in his SUV. Gopher Gas, which is located right near his house, sells gas for $3.58 a gallon. Around the corner, Franklin Gas sells gas for $3.61 a gallon. If Ben has to fill his tank twice a month, how much money will he save in a year by purchasing gas from Gopher Gas every time?
   a. $12.24
   b. $12.50
   c. $14.20
   d. $14.40

3. What is the unit price of T-shirts that cost $48.60 for 3-dozen shirts?
   a. $16.20
   b. $1.62
   c. $1.35
   d. $1.12

4. Jordan's car gets 35 mpg on a 16-gallon tank of gas. If Jordan is taking a trip that is 1,425 miles long, how many times will he have to refill his tank before he reaches his destination, assuming that he begins the trip with a full tank of gas?
   a. 1
   b. 2
   c. 3
   d. 4

5. A sedan travels 516 miles on a 16-gallon tank of gas. An SUV hybrid travels 445 miles on a 14-gallon tank of gas. Which car is more gas efficient?
   a. Sedan
   b. SUV Hybrid

LESSON 1.3 ACTIVITY
A Healthier Percent

Directions: How healthy is your diet? In this activity, you are going to compare your current diet with that recommended by health and nutritional professionals. Then, after you have calculated the breakdown of your current calorie intake, you will make a food plan that falls in line with percentages recommended by doctors and nutritionists.

1. Over the course of 1–2 weeks, fill out the Food Tracker Handout by making a list of the current foods you eat, the number of calories (best estimate) of each food item consumed, and the category (fruits, vegetables, proteins, grains, and dairy) that the item falls under. Only list the foods that you would typically eat on a week-by-week basis. If you attend a birthday party and have cake, that would not necessarily fall under a normal food habit. Also, if you get a large bucket of popcorn at the movies one weekend, that doesn't need to be listed unless you go to the movies consistently week to week.

2. In class, using your Calorie Calculations Worksheet, total up the number of calories you eat in a week as well as the specific breakdown of calories per food group. Then, using your knowledge of calculating percent using rates, calculate the percentage of calories that are vegetables, fruits, proteins, grains, and dairy (show your work using rates).

3. Discuss with your class how your percentages compare with the percentages recommended by doctors and nutritionists. Where are the differences? What foods do you notice that might influence the percentages negatively or positively?

4. Create a food plan using the Food Pyramid Plan Handout. Calculate the total number of calories needed in each category based on the recommended amounts of each of the five food groups. Make a list of foods that you could add to your plan so that you meet the recommended percentages. Discuss with your class and teacher healthier calorie options to substitute for current foods on your list. Use the Healthy Food Options Handout to assist you in making your food plan.

5. Share your food plan with the class and discuss how you calculated your percentages and what food decisions you made based on the evidence and recommendations.

Extend Your Thinking

1. Discuss the foods on your Food Tracker Handout with your partner or group. Discuss which foods would fall under "good" foods and which could be labeled as "bad" foods. Calculate the percentage of foods that are "good" foods and the percentage of "bad" foods.

2. Compare your Food Tracker Handout with your Food Plan Handout. Make a note of the areas in which you made changes to your current diet. Calculate the percentage increase and percentage decrease of calories made to your current diet. For example, if you currently only eat 150 calories of vegetables each week, but you changed that to 450 calories each week in your Food Plan, you would calculate the percentage increase from 150 to 450 as a 200% increase in vegetable calories.

3. Using the percentages that you calculated in Extension 1, figure out how you would have to alter your diet so that the foods you eat would fall into the healthy category. Determine by how many calories in certain areas you need to increase or decrease your diet in order to maintain a healthy diet. Calculate that percent increase and decrease of these changes. Base your decisions on the percentage of carbohydrates, proteins, and fats that you should have in your diet on a daily basis.

LESSON 1.3 PRACTICE
Calculate the Percent

Directions: Complete the problems below.

1. On a specialized food plan designed by her nutritionist, Maria noticed that 40% of her diet needed to be vegetables. Currently she is consuming 375 calories in vegetables per day on her 2,500-calorie diet.
   a. What is the current percentage of her diet that is made up of vegetables?

   b. How many more vegetable calories does she need to add to her diet to get to 40%?

   c. Maria decides to buy a bag of baby carrots to increase the vegetables in her diet. She reads that a serving of baby carrots is 40 calories. If she has $4\frac{1}{2}$ servings of carrots, what percentage of her additional vegetable calories (from Part B) does she consume?

2. A farmer is planting his crops at the beginning of spring. He wants to devote 24% of his acreage to green beans. His sets aside an additional 50% of his crops for corn.
   a. If the remaining acreage of his farm is for tomatoes, what percentage of his crops will be tomatoes?

   b. If the farmer owns 60 acres of land, how many acres are set aside for each crop?

   c. A late freeze kills a quarter of the corn that the farmer planted. How many acres of corn are remaining after the freeze?

d. The farmer makes $5,000 an acre for the green beans, $10,000 an acre for the corn, and $8,000 an acre for the tomatoes. What percentage of his total earnings comes from his tomato harvest? Assume that the number of acres of green beans and tomatoes comes from Part B and the number of acres of corn comes from Part C.

Extend Your Thinking

1. The next time you go to the grocery store, make a list of foods (no more than four) that you think have the best good-calorie per cost ratio. Determine the healthiest items that you can buy at the grocery for the cheapest price. For example, which foods give you the most amount of nutrition for the cheapest price?

LESSON 1.3

Assessment Practice

Directions: Complete the problems below.

1. Benjamin purchased 150 of the 200 available chickens from the farm. What percentage of the chickens did he buy?
   a. 30%
   b. 60%
   c. 75%
   d. 85%

2. If Jody ordered 55% of the 400 bolts of fabric from her supplier, how many bolts of fabric did she order?
   a. 110
   b. 220
   c. 300
   d. 330

3. Miles had completed 25% of his race by 10 a.m. If he had already run 3 miles, how many miles did he have remaining?
   a. 4
   b. 8
   c. 9
   d. 12

4. Only 30% of a 20-gallon tank of water is filled. If a valve pumps water into the tank at 2 quarts every 15 minutes, how many hours will it take for the tank to fill completely?
   a. 7
   b. 10
   c. 14
   d. 28

5. A farmer receives $0.72 for every ear of corn that he harvests. His main crop comes from an acre of farmland just north of his house. If the farmer is able to harvest the entire acre, he gets 5,000 ears of corn. If he received $2,484 from his crop this year, what percentage of his crop did he harvest successfully?
   a. 35%
   b. 44%
   c. 60%
   d. 69%

LESSON 1.4 ACTIVITY
Converting Units Taboo

Directions: You and your partner are competing in a game of Converting Units Taboo (CUT) with another pair of students.

1. Shuffle your stack of CUT Cards.

2. The group with the oldest player goes first.

3. One student will then draw a CUT Card.

4. This student will try to get their partner to guess the value on the card by giving equivalent values without using the taboo unit. For example, the card might read 36 inches and the taboo unit might be feet. The student might give their partner this hint without using the taboo unit: "This value is equivalent to 1 yard, and you would probably use this unit to measure the length of a pencil." The student also could have said, "This unit of measurement can be converted into yards" or "This unit of measurement is found on a ruler." Be creative as you think of your clues.

5. If you were assigned to use the required word part of the card, the clue-giver has to incorporate that word or phrase into their hint in some way. For example, if the required word is yards, you must use the yards conversion in your hint.

6. Both the clue-giver and the guesser need to complete their Converting Units Taboo Worksheet where they show their conversion work using ratios. For example, the clue-giver receives a CUT Card that shows 36 inches but they cannot use the word *feet*. In the hint blank, the clue-giver will write yards, miles, or centimeters as possible units to use in his hint. The clue-giver will then make the conversions to find out how many yards, miles, or centimeters are equivalent to 36 inches.

   When the guesser receives the hint, they will write the possible units that the card might be. So in this case, the guesser might have guessed inches or feet depending on the clue (this can be changed as the clue-giver makes corrections based on incorrect guesses). For example, if the guesser receives the hint that this value will be equivalent to 1 yard, the guesser will then convert 1 yard into the units that they think is correct and proceed to guess that as the value on the card. If the guess is incorrect, the clue-giver can give the guesser more hints.

7. Groups will see how many cards they can guess correctly in 5 minutes. While one team is competing, the other team needs to be checking its math and guesses to make sure the team giving the clues and guessing is getting it correct.

8. Then the other group will take its turn to see if it can guess more.

Extend Your Thinking

1. Now that you have played the game, create your own taboo cards with unit values and taboo units that cannot be used in the conversion hints.

LESSON 1.4

Converting Units Taboo Cards

96 inches	4 miles	2 gallons
Taboo Word: Feet	**Taboo Word:** Feet	**Taboo Word:** Quarts
Required Hint: _____	**Required Hint:** _____	**Required Hint:** _____
16 yards	2 hours	8 weeks
Taboo Word: Feet	**Taboo Word:** Minutes	**Taboo Word:** Days
Required Hint: _____	**Required Hint:** _____	**Required Hint:** _____
5 liters	8 meters	9 kilometers
Taboo Word: Milliliters	**Taboo Word:** Centimeters	**Taboo Word:** Meters
Required Hint: _____	**Required Hint:** _____	**Required Hint:** _____
15 milliliters	24 inches	0.5 miles
Taboo Word: Liters	**Taboo Word:** Feet	**Taboo Word:** Feet
Required Hint: _____	**Required Hint:** _____	**Required Hint:** _____

LESSON 1.4

Converting Units Taboo Worksheet

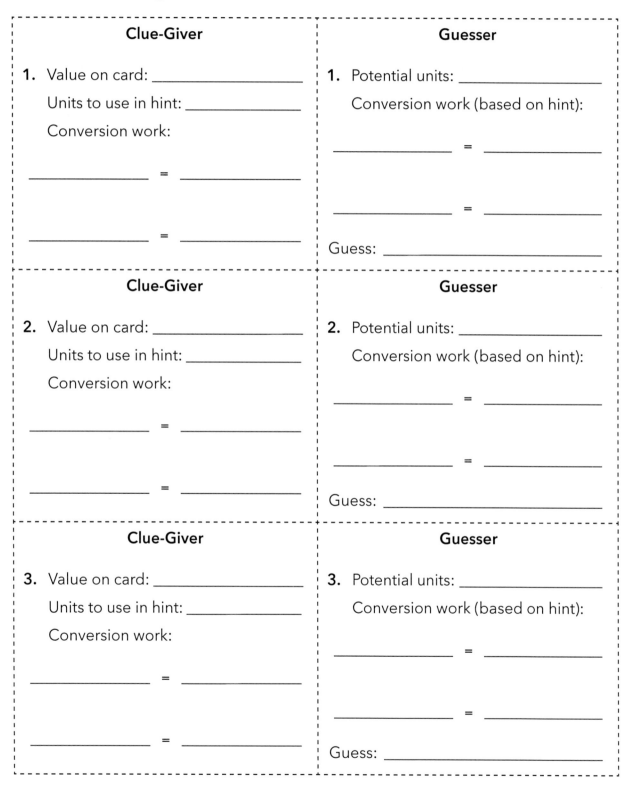

Clue-Giver

1. Value on card: _____

   Units to use in hint: _____

   Conversion work:

   _____ = _____

   _____ = _____

Guesser

1. Potential units: _____

   Conversion work (based on hint):

   _____ = _____

   _____ = _____

   Guess: _____

Clue-Giver

2. Value on card: _____

   Units to use in hint: _____

   Conversion work:

   _____ = _____

   _____ = _____

Guesser

2. Potential units: _____

   Conversion work (based on hint):

   _____ = _____

   _____ = _____

   Guess: _____

Clue-Giver

3. Value on card: _____

   Units to use in hint: _____

   Conversion work:

   _____ = _____

   _____ = _____

Guesser

3. Potential units: _____

   Conversion work (based on hint):

   _____ = _____

   _____ = _____

   Guess: _____

Section I: Ratios and Proportional Relationships

LESSON 1.4

Blank Taboo Cards

_____ (value, include units) **Taboo Word:** _____	_____ (value, include units) **Taboo Word:** _____	_____ (value, include units) **Taboo Word:** _____
_____ (value, include units) **Taboo Word:** _____	_____ (value, include units) **Taboo Word:** _____	_____ (value, include units) **Taboo Word:** _____
_____ (value, include units) **Taboo Word:** _____	_____ (value, include units) **Taboo Word:** _____	_____ (value, include units) **Taboo Word:** _____
_____ (value, include units) **Taboo Word:** _____	_____ (value, include units) **Taboo Word:** _____	_____ (value, include units) **Taboo Word:** _____

LESSON 1.4 PRACTICE
Converting Units

Directions: Complete the problems below.

1. Joshua works at an aquarium store in his hometown. The manager asks him to empty and refill all of the display aquariums in the store. Joshua uses a 1-quart bucket to fill each aquarium.
   a. If each aquarium needs to have exactly 10 gallons of water, how many times will he need to fill his bucket to fill the aquarium?

   b. Joshua times himself. He realizes that he can fill the 1-quart bucket in 15 seconds. If there are 40 aquariums to be refilled, how many minutes will it take him to fill every display aquarium in the store?

   c. After Joshua has filled all of the aquariums, another employee puts the fish in the tanks. Joshua is in charge of getting the food together for the fish. Joshua knows that each fish in the tank gets 1 teaspoon of food per day. If Joshua uses 35 cups of food over a week, how many fish are there in the store?

2. A distance runner, Selene, is running across the country from Boston to San Francisco for charity. The distance from Boston to San Francisco is 3,100 miles.
   a. Selene runs exactly 200 miles a week. If she has already run for 10 weeks, how many days does she have left until she reaches San Francisco?

   b. Selene's best friend is the CEO of a major U.S. company. His company pledged to donate $0.01 for every foot that she ran. How much has she earned so far in the 10 weeks that she has run?

c. Selene limits herself to 10 hours of running per day. How fast is she running in miles per hour?

Extend Your Thinking

1. How fast do you travel on your way home from school? Make a note of the distance (in miles) from your school to your home and the time (in hours) that it takes you to get home. This number will probably be a decimal. Calculate the average miles per hour at which you travel during your drive. Then, convert your average speed into kilometers per hour and feet per second. Use a calculator to assist in your calculations. Round all answers to the nearest hundredth.

Average speed	Calculations	Kilometers per hour	Feet per second

LESSON 1.4

Assessment Practice

Directions: Complete the problems below.

1. A tank can hold 36 liters of water. If a valve pumps 3,000 mL of water into the tank every 30 minutes, how many hours will it take to fill the tank completely?
   a. 4
   b. 6
   c. 8
   d. 10

2. Mike's car broke down 5 miles from the auto shop. If he can push his car 1,056 feet per hour, how many hours will it take him to reach the auto shop?
   a. 25
   b. 30
   c. 35
   d. 40

3. A professional football wide receiver totaled 1,543 yards receiving during the 2014 season. How many feet is this receiving total?
   a. 2,975
   b. 3,765
   c. 4,235
   d. 4,629

4. Jules earned $360 working a 40-hour week at the local diner. How much money did she earn per minute?
   a. $0.12
   b. $0.14
   c. $0.15
   d. $0.18

5. Harold earns $11.50 an hour. If he works 35 hours a week for 50 weeks, how much money does Harold earn in one year?
   a. $12,150
   b. $20,125
   c. $25, 275
   d. $30,500

LESSON 2.1 ACTIVITY
Fractions of a Class Change

Directions: How fair is your school's tardy policy? Do you think you and your class-mates have enough time between classes? In this activity, you are about to prove it one way or another. Partner up with one of your classmates and begin working on a reasonable time to take when changing classes.

1. Measure the length of one of your (and your partner's) typical stride from the heel of one shoe to the toe of the other shoe. Write the length of this step in inches as a whole number (rounding if necessary), a decimal, and a fraction.

Your Stride (In Inches)	
a. Whole number:	_____
b. Decimal:	_____
c. Fraction:	_____

Your Partner's Stride (In Inches)	
a. Whole number:	_____
b. Decimal:	_____
c. Fraction:	_____

2. Make a list of class changes you have throughout the day. Choose two class changes (one of yours and one of your partner's). Use the premeasured pieces of string provided by your teacher to measure the distance from one class to the next. Figure out the total distance between each class change (in feet and in inches) and write it as a whole number (rounding if necessary), a decimal, and a fraction.

Your Class Change From _____ to _____	
In Feet	
a. Whole number:	_____
b. Decimal:	_____
c. Fraction:	_____
In Inches	
a. Whole number:	_____
b. Decimal:	_____
c. Fraction:	_____

Your Partner's Change From _____ to _____	
In Feet	
a. Whole number:	_____
c. Decimal:	_____
c. Fraction:	_____
In Inches	
a. Whole number:	_____
b. Decimal:	_____
c. Fraction:	_____

3. Figure out how many steps it will take you to move between classes (for both class changes) and write your answer as a whole number, a decimal, and a fraction.

Your Class Change From _____ to _____	
In Number of Steps	
a. Whole number:	_____
b. Decimal:	_____
c. Fraction:	_____

Your Partner's Change From _____ to _____	
In Number of Steps	
a. Whole number:	_____
b. Decimal:	_____
c. Fraction:	_____

4. Figure out how many steps you can take in 5 seconds with a typical pace: _____ . Using that number, calculate how many seconds it will take you to make the class change. Write your answer as a whole number, a fraction, and a decimal.

Your Class Change From _____ to _____	
In Seconds	
a. Whole number:	_____
b. Decimal:	_____
c. Fraction:	_____

Your Partner's Change From _____ to _____	
In Seconds	
a. Whole number:	_____
b. Decimal:	_____
c. Fraction:	_____

5. Determine whether or not you have enough time between classes based on your calculations. Explain your answer.

Extend Your Thinking

1. Imagine that your principal is trying to put together schedules for the next school year. He wants student input on the different class changes that students might struggle to make in the allotted amount of time. With your partner, hypothesize and test different paths that students might take that would require a longer time than the amount allotted for class changes at your school. Show your calculations and write a brief petition to present your findings to your principal to make your case.

2. Calculate the distance you can travel by jogging for 5 seconds. Make a comparison between your typical pace and your jogging pace. Compare using a time period of 10 minutes. How much farther could you run than walk in 10 minutes? As a class, make a note of each of your different jogging times. If each person in the class were part of a relay team and each person jogged for 10 minutes, how far would the total distance traveled be for each student in your class put together?

LESSON 2.1 PRACTICE
Applications Using Fractions and Decimals

Directions: Complete the problems below.

1. A farmer goes to a carpenter's workshop looking for fence posts. The carpenter shows him all 80 of the fence posts in his shop.

   a. The farmer tells the carpenter he will buy $\frac{4}{5}$ of the fence posts. How many fence posts did he buy?

   b. Each fence post is 4 feet high. The farmer measures and realizes he needs to cut 8.5 inches off the end of each post. How long is each post after the cut? Challenge: Write your measurement in inches and feet.

   c. The farmer's plan is to fence in a strip of his land for herding his cattle so that it forms a square. He decides to place the four corner posts of the fence and then place 15 posts in between each corner post so that there is a distance of $8\frac{1}{8}$ feet between each post around the entire fenced in area. Calculate the area and the perimeter of this fenced in area.

2. A deliveryman earns $0.75 for every mile that he drives.

   a. If the deliveryman has driven 45 and $\frac{3}{5}$ miles so far this morning, how much money has he earned?

   b. The deliveryman is trying to save his money to take his wife on a vacation. He calculates that he needs to earn $150 a day to save up for their vacation and pay for living expenses. How many more miles does he need to drive today to earn his $150?

c. The deliveryman and his wife worked out that he needs to set aside 18% of the $150 each day to fund their vacation. If he has been saving for 3 weeks (driving 5 days a week), how much has he saved?

d. The deliveryman had engine trouble one week and didn't get to save as much as he wanted that week. With the engine fixed, he has 5 days left until the vacation date. He still needs $210 dollars to meet his vacation budget. What percent of the $150 does he need to set aside each day this week (5 days) to meet his goal?

Extend Your Thinking

1. More and more health and fitness sites are suggesting that people walk 10,000 steps a day to maintain a healthy, active lifestyle. Using the normal pace that you calculated during Activity 2.1, figure out how long it would take you to walk 10,000 steps. How much total distance will you travel if you walk 10,000 steps?

2. Some physical education classes use pedometers in their lessons. Use a pedometer to see how many steps you take during a typical day and calculate the additional time and distance you would need to travel to reach the 10,000 step goal.

LESSON 2.1

Assessment Practice

Directions: Complete the problems below.

1. A recipe for brownies requires $4\frac{1}{2}$ cups of sugar and makes enough brownies for 12 people. If Yousef only wants to make brownies for 8 people, how many cups of sugar will he need for the recipe?
    a. 9 cups
    b. $2\frac{1}{8}$ cups
    c. 3 cups
    d. 8 cups

2. A relay race was $\frac{4}{5}$ of a mile long. If each person on the relay team had to run $\frac{1}{10}$ of a mile, how many people were on each relay team?
    a. 4
    b. 8
    c. 10
    d. 12

3. A farmer sections off 80% of his 20.45-acre farm for cotton. How many acres of cotton did he plant?
    a. 16.36 acres
    b. 4.09 acres
    c. 16.5 acres
    d. 18.24 acres

4. A pair of socks requires 0.75 feet of fabric to make. If a clothing manufacturer has 60.25 feet of fabric, how many socks can the manufacturer make?
    a. 80 socks
    b. 80.33 socks
    c. 45 socks
    d. 81 socks

5. A warehouse has 1,235 boxes of envelopes. Each delivery truck can hold 85 boxes of envelopes. How many trucks does the warehouse need to hire to ship all of its envelopes?
    a. 14 trucks
    b. 15 trucks
    c. 16 trucks
    d. 17 trucks

LESSON 2.2 ACTIVITY
Creating Monster Multiples

Directions: Mad scientists wanted! You are needed to create a monster number for a new zoo opening in your area. Because you have a great understanding of a number's DNA, the zoo needs you to create a monster number by combining two or more numbers' DNA.

1. Your teacher will assign you one number, most likely a two- or three-digit number that you might find in the wild. Create a DNA map of the number by completing a prime factorization for your number. Complete Lesson 2.2 Number DNA handout to record your scientific findings.

2. Compare the DNA map of your number to that of the other mad scientists around you (your classmates). Find numbers that share a common factor or GCF. You and your partner will then "splice" the unique DNA of one number (all of the prime factors left after the GCF is taken out) with the unique DNA of the other number to create a monster multiple.

3. When you have created your monster multiple, design a monster to represent this monster multiple using your construction paper.

4. Create a zoo identification card using Lesson 2.2 Zoo Identification Cards handout. Identify the GCF of the two numbers you spliced and the unique DNA that you combined to form your monster. For example, 36 and 48 share a GCF of 12. The unique DNA left would be 3 and 4, respectively. The zoo identification card would be 12 (3 x 4) to indicate that 12 is the DNA shared and that 3 and 4 are the unique DNA spliced together to create the monster multiple of 144. Then write a brief description of your Monster Multiple: natural habitats, types of behaviors your multiple might exhibit, and so forth (be creative!).

5. Group your numbers into common exhibits by displaying the numbers who share the monster multiples that share the same GCFs.

Extend Your Thinking

1. You can "visit" the zoo by walking around and looking at the identification cards. You should try to notice patterns in each of the different species (numbers who share the same GCF). Generalize a rule for numbers who share the same GCFs. For example, you might notice that monster numbers formed between numbers who share the GCF of 15 will end in either a 5 or a 0. Try to make connections between the patterns that you notice and the GCF of the monster numbers.

Math Curriculum for Gifted Students, Grade 6, Sections I–II

2. Some monster numbers may be caught in the wild and brought to the zoo for safekeeping. It is your job to correctly classify these wild monster numbers. You will receive four- and five-digit numbers and break down each number's DNA to find in which GCF section of the zoo the number should go and what two numbers were spliced together to form the monster number (with some numbers the answers might vary and you can discuss why that is).

LESSON 2.2
Number DNA

First Number: _____

List of prime numbers that make up the "DNA" of your number (list repeated prime numbers). Construct a factor tree in the space below (other methods can also be substituted).

Number DNA (prime factorization of your number): _____

LESSON 2.2
Zoo Identification Cards

Monster Multiple 1

(Picture Here)	Name:
	Species (common GCF):
	DNA Makeup (GCF and product of unique DNA):
Description:	

Monster Multiple 2

(Picture Here)	Name:
	Species (common GCF):
	DNA Makeup (GCF and product of unique DNA):
Description:	

LESSON 2.2 PRACTICE
Factors and Multiples

Directions: Complete the problems below.

1. A baker has 45 muffins and 60 rolls. He wants to make bags of muffins and rolls so that each bag has the same number of muffins and the same number of rolls with none being left over.
   a. What are the possible numbers of bags he can make?

   b. What is the greatest number of bags he can make?

   c. How many muffins and rolls will be in each bag if he makes the greatest number of bags possible?

2. Judith and Augustina are running laps around the lake. They both start at the same time and go in the same direction. Judith completes a lap every 4 minutes and Augustina completes a lap every 6 minutes.
   a. If they just started, how many minutes will it be before they are both at the starting line at the same time again?

   b. If they both run for 60 minutes, how many times will they meet up at the starting line during their run?

   c. During that 60-minute time period, how many laps will Judith have run and how many laps will Augustina have run?

Extend Your Thinking

1. It is your job to create a taxonomy of monster numbers. Be as creative as you like in your classifications. For example, all numbers have a factor of 1, so that might be the kingdom in which all monster numbers are classified. You can then group numbers into phylum, class, order, family, genus, and species as you see fit. You can then compare your classification systems to each other and see where you agreed and differed. Discuss the reasons why you chose your classification system with other groups in your class.

LESSON 2.2

Assessment Practice

Directions: Complete the problems below.

1. A florist is making flower bouquets out of pink and purple roses. The florist has 80 pink roses and 120 purple roses. What is the greatest number of bouquets the florist can make so that each bouquet has the same number of pink and purple roses and no roses are left over?
   a. 12
   b. 20
   c. 40
   d. 80

2. What is the smallest possible number that is divisible by both 16 and 24?
   a. 16
   b. 24
   c. 36
   d. 48

3. Justin goes hiking every 8 days. Joel goes hiking every 10 days. If they just hiked together on the same day, how many days will it be before they both hike on the same day again?
   a. 2 days
   b. 40 days
   c. 80 days
   d. 120 days

4. The Necklace Depot sells necklace charms in packs of 10. The Lovely Necklace sells necklace charms in packs of 15. At the end of the day, both stores sold the same number of necklace charms. Which of the following could be the number of charms they sold that day?
   a. 20
   b. 45
   c. 160
   d. 330

5. Horace has 50 pens and 75 pencils. He wants to make packs of writing utensils so that each pack has the same number of pens and the same number of pencils while making sure to use all of the pens and pencils available. If Horace made the greatest possible number of packs of pencils and pens, how many pencils were in each pack?

   a. 3
   b. 5
   c. 10
   d. 25

LESSON 2.3 ACTIVITY
Positive and Negative Narrative

Directions: Think you can find the positives and negatives in a poem? Sure, it's easy to find what you like and dislike, but can you track a number throughout a poem and find the language that changes in ways positive or negative? Follow the directions below.

1. Read Lesson 2.3 Positive and Negative Narrative Poem. Highlight (in different colors) language in the poem that signifies positive and negative values or changes to a number.

2. Complete Lesson 2.3 Narrative Poem Worksheet.

Extend Your Thinking

1. Create a number line to track the movements of two of the numbers (one positive, one negative) throughout the length of the narrative poem or short story that you write. Use a green marker to track positive changes and a red marker to track negative changes. Circle with a blue marker the point(s) when there are two points on the number line that are opposites.

2. Look through your number line and turn the positive and negative movements of the numbers into addition and subtraction operations. Write the operations with the starting number and the movement (positive or negative) and the resulting number. For example, if a temperature (in Celsius) starts at negative 14 (-14) and drops 4 degrees, the operation would be -14 – 4 = -18 degrees. After writing the operations out, try to generalize rules about adding and subtracting with negative numbers.

LESSON 2.3
Positive and Negative Narrative Poem

Directions: As you read the poem, highlight words that indicate positive or negative temperatures.

The sun splintered down on the tundra below
A warmth filled the air and the temperature rose
It climbed and it climbed some 15 degrees
There was hardly a sign of the danger, the freeze.
Bartholomew worked in his Antarctic lab
Testing the ice, slab after slab
Bristled and burned, his fingers afire
He was beginning to slow; he was beginning to tire
Careless, an ice block fell to the floor
It shattered and fractured into pieces galore
Out of the core of ice rose a harsh scream
And the pieces that scattered all melted to steam
The lights in the lab went instantly black
The temperature plunged 40 degrees with a crack
Bartholomew, frightened, threw on his jacket
And ran out the door to escape all the racket
By the time he looked up the sun was scarce to be found
His feet slipped and he slid over the ice-covered ground
Shaking all over, he looked with a shock
The temperature outside had dropped like a rock
Well below zero, it continued to fall
It fell 30 degrees before beginning to stall
Worn down and wearied he ran from the air
He started a fire with one of his flares
With the flame from the flare he warmed up his toes
He heated his hands and thawed out his nose
The air warmed around him from the heat and the glow
Twenty-five degrees warmer though still very low
Bartholomew saw and realized with fear
The flare's light was waning and the warmth's end was near.
Before the light faded he looked at his gauge
"Seventy-five below zero," he read with great rage
The dark closed around him and he let out a scream
He woke with a start and realized it was all just a dream
Bartholomew read the thermometer clear
It read 75 degrees, and he shouted a cheer.

LESSON 2.3

Narrative Poem Worksheet

Directions: Use the narrative poem to answer Questions 1–3.

1. **a.** What were some of the highlighted words in the poem that indicated positive or negative temperatures?

   b. How did you know they indicated positive or negative temperatures?

2. Write the temperatures in the poem as integer values. On the poem, track the numbers as they increase or decrease based on positive or negative wording.

3. Make notes as the numbers change and mark the resolution of the story when the numbers become opposites. Which values in the poem were opposites? Explain how you know they are opposites.

4. Now it is your turn. Think of real-life situations (or fantastical situations) where positive and negative numbers can be used. What is the topic on which your want to write your narrative poem or short story?

5. Brainstorm a storyline that can incorporate those real-life situations into the plot. List some keywords related to your topic that indicate positive or negative values. For example, if you are using temperature, you can use words like falling, rising, cooling, or warming in your story.

Positive: **Negative:**

6. Write your own narrative poem or short story where the negative and positive integers change as part of the story's conflict or based on the characters in the story and their actions. Use different terminology in your story to indicate positive and negative changes to numbers.

7. As a resolution, you should have at least one pair of integers become opposites as a result of the plot of the story. For example, at the end of a story, a bird might rise to a height of 35 m and a dolphin might dive to 35 m below sea level (or -35 m), which is where the story would end.

LESSON 2.3 PRACTICE

Using Positive and Negative Numbers

Directions: Complete the problems below.

1. On a climb of K2, the mountaineers began their day 22,450 feet above sea level. They made an ascent of 1,500 feet before descending to 21,250 feet to acclimatize.
   a. Assign an integer value to their ascent and descent.

   b. Calculate the net gain/loss of altitude on this day of climbing.

   c. The climbers spend the next 5 days ascending from 21,250 feet to 26,500 feet. What was the average ascent per day during this stretch?

   d. The climbers then summit to 28,251 feet. They spend the next 30 minutes at the summit before descending back down the mountain to 26,500 feet. What was the net gain of altitude during this climb?

   e. The next day the climbers descend to 20,500 feet. What integer can represent this descent?

2. Camille opened a bank account and deposited $1,500.
   a. Write this value as an integer.

   b. Camille spends $750 on a plane ticket to Paris, France. How much money does she have in her account now? Represent this purchase as an integer value.

   c. She decides to spend $250 a night on a hotel for 5 nights. Write an integer value to represent the value of her bank account now.

Extend Your Thinking

1. Research the average high and low temperature for a month in your town. This should be one monthly high and one monthly low (calculate the average if needed). Track the current temperature over a week and compare it to the average monthly temperature using positive and negative numbers. As you assign a positive or negative number to each temperature, create a bar graph to represent the current temperature as it compares to the average. Consider the x-axis (horizontal axis) of your bar graph to be the average monthly temperature. Negative values should fall below that line, while positive values should be above that line.

LESSON 2.3

Assessment Practice

Directions: Complete the problems below.

1. If Galen has less than -$30 on his credit card, which of the following values can represent the amount of money he has?
   a. -$25
   b. $25
   c. $35
   d. -$42

2. Jonathan starts from his house and travels east 35.8 miles. He then travels west 42.2 miles. How far is he from his house?
   a. 6.4 miles
   b. 78 miles
   c. -7.6 miles
   d. 7.6 miles

3. Charlotte is diving from a 30-foot-high diving board. What integer value can represent the distance from the surface of the water she needs to reach to be opposite of the height of the diving board?
   a. -30 feet
   b. 30 feet
   c. 15 feet
   d. 60 feet

4. Which of the following situations would not represent -5?
   a. A temperature fall of 5 degrees
   b. A deposit of $5
   c. A loss by 5 points
   d. Snorkeling 5 feet underwater

5. Starting from an elevation of 45 degrees below sea level a diver rose 30 feet. Represent the diver's new elevation as an integer.
   a. 15
   b. -15
   c. 75
   d. -75

LESSON 2.4 ACTIVITY
Mapping a Novel

Directions: How well do you know your favorite book? Can you visualize all of the important locations of this book? Create a map of the central setting to your favorite book by plotting the important points on a coordinate grid based on text evidence from the book. This coordinate map should help a future reader better visualize the events of the book as the character(s) move from one place to the next.

1. Determine the central location or most important location in your story (or in the part of your story on which you are focusing). This is the origin on your coordinate plane. For example, if you are reading a Harry Potter novel, the central location might be Hogwarts School of Witchcraft and Wizardry (or a specific area inside the castle).
2. Determine 7–10 specific locations to which the character(s) travel that are located around your central location. Use context clues from the book to determine a direction and distance from your central location at which this point is located. Try to simplify directions to varying degrees of north, south, east, and west.
3. Using your direction and distance relative to the origin, plot each specific location on your Lesson 2.4 Coordinate Grid Setting Map worksheet as a point with a specific ordered pair.
4. To identify each specific location, list the ordered pair, a name for the location, and a brief text description of the location for each point on your map (including the origin). For example, you might identify the origin as (0, 0) as Hogwarts and a brief text description about the castle.
5. Complete your Lesson 2.4 Setting Map worksheet by identifying specific locations and their ordered pairs and using absolute value to calculate the distances between points on your map.
6. Keep in mind that locations on your map could be related to an event or conflict in the story and not necessarily linked to a specific landmark.

Extend Your Thinking

1. Think about which unit of measure would be appropriate for determining the distance between the points on your map and create a scale to represent that unit of measure. This will, of course, be an estimate, but you should try to use your scale to make an educated guess for how far the character traveled during the story in the book. If you only focused on a specific set of chapters in the book, you can limit your distance-traveled calculations to that part of the book.
2. Look through the descriptions in the story as a character is moving from one point to another. Make a note of parts of imagery that are mentioned in this journey. Add these images to your Lesson 2.4 Setting Map worksheet using fraction or decimal ordered pairs and calculate the corresponding distances between major points on your map and these newly added descriptions.

LESSON 2.4
Coordinate Grid Setting Map

Directions: Using the coordinate grid below, represent a point on the grid for every important location/event in the novel you are reading.

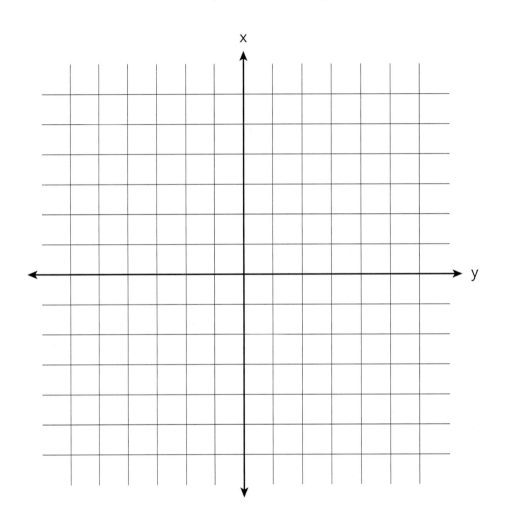

Math Curriculum for Gifted Students, Grade 6, Sections I–II

LESSON 2.4
Setting Map

Directions: Use the coordinate grid you made on the Lesson 2.4 Coordinate Grid Setting Map handout to complete the following worksheet. List the locations/events you placed on your grid and their corresponding ordered pair. Let Point A be your central location (origin).

Point A: _____ Ordered Pair: (_____ , _____)

Point B: _____ Ordered Pair: (_____ , _____)

Point C: _____ Ordered Pair: (_____ , _____)

Point D: _____ Ordered Pair: (_____ , _____)

Point E: _____ Ordered Pair: (_____ , _____)

Point F: _____ Ordered Pair: (_____ , _____)

Point G: _____ Ordered Pair: (_____ , _____)

1. What is the distance from Point A to Point B? _____

2. What is the distance from Point E to Point G? _____

3. What is the distance from Point C to Point F? _____

4. What is the distance from Point B to Point C? _____

5. At one point in your story's plot, your character probably travels through a series of places or events. Describe the journey that your character takes at one point in the story and then use your corresponding points to calculate the distance your character would have traveled during this journey.

LESSON 2.4 PRACTICE
Coordinate Grids

Directions: Complete the problems below.

1. Caleb is starting a paper route. He sits down at his desk and begins mapping out the route. He starts at his house and travels west 3 blocks. He delivers his first paper to Mrs. Peterson before turning north.

    a. If his house represents the origin on a graph, what ordered pair will represent Mrs. Peterson's house?

    b. Explain how you determined the ordered pair for Part A.

    c. Caleb turns north from Mrs. Peterson's house and travels 5 blocks. During the 5 blocks, he delivers 10 papers. Create ordered pairs that might represent these 10 houses. Justify your answers for these ordered pairs.

    d. Caleb then turns east and travels 5 blocks. If he is finished with his route, write the directions for him to get back to his house from here without turning around and going back the way he came.

e. If each block is 0.25 of a mile, how far does Caleb ride during his route?

2. Porter is marking important locations on a graph. He marks his house at (0, 0). He marks his school at (4, 5). He marks the library at (-3, 6), his favorite restaurant at (-3, -4), and his basketball gym at (0, 6).
   a. If each point on the graph represents one mile, how far is it from his house to the gym?

   b. How far is it from the gym to the library?

   c. How far is it from the library to the restaurant?

   d. If Porter starts at school, then goes to the library, then out to eat, then to the gym, and finally back home, how far does he travel if he can only move up, down, left, or right on the graph?

Extend Your Thinking

1. You have received a map of the continental United States from your teacher. Place a grid over it and plot the major cities on the grid using ordered pairs. Using the scale and the ordered pairs, estimate distances between cities based on absolute value calculations. Compare the estimated distances to the actual distances between the cities. Explain what you think could cause the discrepancies between the estimated distance and the actual distance between cities.

LESSON 2.4

Assessment Practice

Directions: Complete the problems below.

1. On a map, the bank is located at the coordinates (3, 8) and the mall is located at (3, -4). How far is the bank from the mall?
   a. 8 units
   b. 4 units
   c. 3 units
   d. 12 units

2. A hunter sets up camp in the woods. He travels 3 miles east, 5 miles north, and then 2 miles west to his deer stand. If his camp is the origin, on which coordinates is his deer stand?
   a. (1, 5)
   b. (3, 5)
   c. (-2, 3)
   d. (5, 3)

3. In which quadrant is the ordered pair (-5, 12) located?
   a. Quadrant I
   b. Quadrant II
   c. Quadrant III
   d. Quadrant IV

4. A house is located at the point (-2, 8.5) on a coordinate map. Another house is located on the point (-2, -6.25). How far away are the two houses from each other?
   a. -2 units
   b. 2.25 units
   c. 8.5 units
   d. 14.75 units

5. A train's route is mapped out on a coordinate grid. The main train station is located at the origin. Each stop is located every 0.25 units on the coordinate grid. If the train is currently at the point (0, 5) how many stops away from the main train station is it?
   a. 20 stops
   b. 15 stops
   c. 10 stops
   d. 5 stops

LESSON 2.5 ACTIVITY
Absolute Value of a Skyline

Directions: Cities become famous for their skylines. Have you ever seen pictures of New York, Chicago, or even Hong Kong? Clusters of massive skyscrapers that dominate the horizon are a testament to the ingenuity and imagination of the human spirit. But exactly how tall are these buildings, and how does their height relate to the tallest buildings in your town or city? With your partner, you will be choosing a major city from around the world and create a diorama so you can visually represent the relationship between the heights of the buildings.

1. Choose one of the largest cities from around the world, including the United States.

2. Make a list of the top 10 tallest buildings in that city as well as the height of the buildings.

3. Calculate the average height of the 10 buildings you researched. This value is your zero (0) value on your number line.

4. Measure the height of this average on your shoebox to begin your diorama. Use a scale of 1 inch = 100 m or 1 inch = 500 feet (feel free to adjust the scale as needed, just make sure you are consistent). Tie your piece of string/yarn across the face of the box to mark the zero on your number line. Remember, the zero line should be the average height of the 10 buildings.

5. Assign an integer value based on each building's height compared to the average height of all of the buildings. A building that is taller than the average will have a positive number, and a building that is shorter will have a negative number.

6. Build your diorama by constructing models for each of your buildings in your diorama. On each building label the height and show the absolute value of the building based on its distance from the average height. Make sure your buildings are constructed to scale.

7. Complete the Lesson 2.5 Absolute Value Skyline Worksheet.

Extend Your Thinking

1. Compare your diorama and buildings from your skyline to other groups in the class. With the other groups in the class, create a number line that orders the heights of the top three buildings from each group in the class. Make sure you also order the buildings by the assigned integers and compare buildings by how they relate to the average height of the skylines. Notice how the rankings of buildings differ.

2. As a class, measure each person's height in feet (write the numbers as mixed fractions). Find the average height of the class and determine an absolute value for each person in the class. These absolute values should be written as a fraction and as a decimal (rounded to the nearest hundredth if necessary). You can assign a negative absolute value to those students who are shorter than the class average and a positive absolute value for those who are taller. Discuss any observations you and your classmates might have about how to order the absolute value of negative and positive fractions.

LESSON 2.5 ACTIVITY
Absolute Value Skyline Worksheet

Directions: Use your research on your city's skyline to complete the worksheet.

1. List the heights of the tallest 10 buildings in your city.

    1st _____   2nd _____   3rd _____   4th _____   5th _____

    6th _____   7th _____   8th _____   9th _____   10th _____

2. What is the average height of those 10 buildings?

3. Write an absolute value to represent the distance each of the 10 buildings is from the average height.

    1st _____   2nd _____   3rd _____   4th _____   5th _____

    6th _____   7th _____   8th _____   9th _____   10th _____

4. What is the height of the tallest building in your hometown? _____

5. Write an absolute value to represent how your hometown's tallest building compares to the average height of the buildings in the city you researched.

6. Choose the shortest and tallest buildings in your hometown's skyline. Explain how the two absolute values used to represent their respective heights relate to the difference in the two buildings' actual heights.

7. Explain how absolute values might be used to find the difference between a positive and negative number.

LESSON 2.5 PRACTICE
Applications of Absolute Value

Directions: Complete the problems below.

1. The average height in a class of sixth graders is 50.2 inches.
    a. If a student is 58.6 inches tall, what absolute value could be written to represent the distance that his height is from the average in the class?

    b. Another student is 42.7 inches tall. What absolute value could be written to represent the distance she is from the average height in the class?

    c. If a student is 56.8 inches tall, what would be considered her opposite height, using the average heights for the class?

2. Three groups of hikers are on Annapurna trying for a summit bid. Group 1 is at a camp (Camp 3) at 23,354 feet. Group 2 is waiting somewhat higher, planning to try for the summit tomorrow. They are at Camp 4, which is right at 25,500 feet. The third group has left Camp 4 for the summit and is climbing at 26,235 feet.
    a. If Camp 4 is the average starting point for a summit try, write an absolute value to represent the distance each of the three groups is from Camp 4.

Math Curriculum for Gifted Students, Grade 6, Sections I–II

b. Group 3 begins its descent from the summit. When the group members get to 25,854 feet, they are opposite of Group 1 from Camp 4. What is the altitude of Group 1?

c. Group 2 began its summit try that morning. Group 2 reaches the summit of 26,545 feet at 10 a.m. Write an absolute value that represents the distance ascended from Camp 4.

d. At 2 p.m. that same day, the altitude of Group 1 can be written as |-50|, the altitude of Group 2 can be written as |945|, and the altitude of Group 3 can be written as |-1,254|. What are the actual altitudes of all three groups?

Extend Your Thinking

1. Begin by measuring the height from the floor to the ceiling in a room. Your height will serve as the zero value on the number line. Make a list of items that are located below you in the room and above you in the room. Measure the heights of these objects and place them accordingly on the number line where objects that are above you are positive and items below you are negative. When you are measuring items, the assigned number should be determined by the distance that item is from your height (which is serving as zero in this situation) not the distance the item is from the floor. You will then calculate the absolute value of the items after ordering them on the number line, making note of which items are opposites.

LESSON 2.5

Assessment Practice

Directions: Complete the problems below.

1. A submarine is currently cruising at 300 feet below sea level. Which absolute value correctly identifies the distance the submarine is from sea level?
   a. $|300|$
   b. $|-300|$
   c. 300
   d. -300

2. Cody plots two points: (3, 16) and (3, -12). Which of the following two points are the same distance as the two Cody plotted?
   a. (3, 16) and (3, 12)
   b. (15, 6) and (-13, 8)
   c. (12, 10) and (-12, -18)
   d. (0, 20) and (0, -8)

3. The perimeter of a rectangle is 28. The base of the rectangle is formed by Point A (-6, 8) and Point B (4, 8). Which of the following points could form the height of the rectangle?
   a. (8, 8)
   b. (-10, 8)
   c. (4, 12)
   d. (-6, -4)

4. A student is given a piece of graph paper with a point marked at the coordinates (-2, -6). The student is told to draw a line up 9 units and place a point there. What are the coordinate points for the new point?
   a. (-8, 6)
   b. (7, -6)
   c. (-2, 3)
   d. (-2, 15)

5. A student is given a point at the origin and told to form a square by drawing a point four units left of the origin and drawing a point four units down from the origin. What are the coordinate for the fourth point that completes the square?
   a. (4, 4)
   b. (4, -4)
   c. (-4, 4)
   d. (-4, -4)

Math Curriculum for Gifted Students, Grade 6, Sections I–II